MW00440434

Sprint Triathlon Training in 4 Weeks

The Ultimate Sprint Triathlon Training Program

by Kylie Palombella

Table of Contents

Introduction

Welcome! Congratulations on taking the first critical step to completing your first sprint triathlon! Getting this book is a fantastic way to get organized and motivated so that you can tackle your sprint triathlon with success.

A word of caution before we begin: Undertaking a training program for physical activity of any kind should always be done in consultation with your health care professionals. Always consult your doctor before beginning any new exercise program. In addition, if you experience any unusual pain or discomfort while training for your triathlon, be sure to discontinue training and consult your doctor immediately.

That said, have fun!

© Copyright 2014 by LCPublifish LLC - All rights reserved.

This document is geared towards providing reliable information in regards to the topic and issue covered. The publication is sold with the idea that the publisher is not required to render accounting, officially permitted, or otherwise, qualified services. If advice is necessary, legal or professional, a practiced individual in the profession should be ordered.

- From a Declaration of Principles which was accepted and approved equally by a Committee of the American Bar Association and a Committee of Publishers and Associations.

In no way is it legal to reproduce, duplicate, or transmit any part of this document in either electronic means or in printed format. Recording of this publication is strictly prohibited and any storage of this document is not allowed unless with written permission from the publisher. All rights reserved.

The information provided herein is stated to be truthful and consistent, in that any liability, in terms of inattention or otherwise, by any usage or abuse of any policies, processes, or directions contained within is solely and completely the responsibility of the recipient reader. Under no circumstances will any legal responsibility or blame be held against the publisher for any reparation, damages, or monetary loss due to the information herein, either directly or indirectly.

Respective authors own all copyrights not held by the publisher.

The information herein is offered for informational purposes solely, and is universal as so. The presentation of the information is without contract or any type of guarantee assurance.

The trademarks that are used are without any consent, and the publication of the trademark is without permission or backing by the trademark owner. All trademarks and brands within this book are for clarifying purposes only and are the owned by the owners themselves, not affiliated with this document.

Chapter 1: A Primer on Triathlons

Triathlons are one of the greatest tests of fitness that a person can face. Typically speaking, a triathlon is a combination of three separate endurance events. In the modern world, triathlons consist of a running, cycling and swimming portion.

Triathlons come in four different lengths. The longest type of triathlon is known colloquially as the "Ironman". This is an incredibly tough race, considered one of the absolute most difficult athletic competitions around. There are few greater tests of a person's endurance, mental toughness and overall physical condition. In an Ironman triathlon, participants run a full marathon, cycle for 112 miles and swim for 2.4 miles.

Only slightly easier is the "long course" or the "half-ironman" triathlon. In this race, the distance of each portion of the Ironman course is cut exactly in half. However, this is still an extreme test of endurance.

The Olympic distance triathlon is more accessible to a wider range of athletes than the more extreme endurance events. In an Olympic triathlon, the swim is under a mile, the cycling portion is only 25 miles and the run is 6.2 miles.

Finally, the shortest distance of triathlon is known as a 'sprint' triathlon, and is the focus of this book. Make no mistake, the sprint triathlon is still a test of fitness, endurance and focus. However, the length of each section makes it much more accessible to the beginning athlete. Even competitors at an early stage of fitness training can, with four weeks of hard work, get themselves ready for a sprint triathlon.

In a sprint triathlon, the participants have to swim for .47 miles. Then they hop on their bikes and cover 12 miles by bicycle before finishing off with a 3.1 mile run. The distances are short, but combined they still represent a significant outpouring of effort.

Chapter 2: Keys to Success

So what are the keys to completing your first sprint triathlon? Well, the first is that you have to dedicate yourself to your training. You can't just jump in and expect to complete a triathlon on day 1. We've put together a comprehensive one month (4-week) training program that is designed to take you from beginner to triathlete, but you have to buy into the process and put in the time.

Training isn't just about getting out of bed and doing your exercise. It is also about eating right, treating your body right and getting your mind right before your first triathlon. This book promises to get you ready, which means that we have to look at all those aspects of preparation as well.

The book starts with a section on nutrition. The food you put in your body is like the fuel that feeds the engine of your car. If you take a $100,000 sports car and put discount fuel in it, it's going to run poorly, consume more gas and lose horsepower. If you put top-shelf, high-octane fuel in it though, it's a world class automobile. We need to make sure that we're putting nothing but high-octane fuel in your engine.

After that, we're going to get into the nitty gritty of

your first two weeks of training. Then we'll take a brief break (in the book, you don't get a break from training!) To discuss mental matters relating to triathlon training. We placed this chapter in the middle but, really, it applies to all stages of your training, so if you want to jump ahead and read it right after you begin the training, go ahead!

Finally, we'll conclude your training, and take a brief look at prepping for race day and what comes after. Hopefully, your journey to your first sprint triathlon is an exciting, challenging and fulfilling one.

Let's get started!

Chapter 3: Nutrition Primer: Fueling the Triathlete Inside

Did you know that there is a triathlete inside you? Well there is, and he or she is just dying to get out. However, to unleash the creature who can bike, swim and run like a champ, you need to feed it correctly.

Diet plans and regimens don't work. That's been proven again and again, and almost every strict, restrictive diet plan on the market has been debunked or failed more than once. This is because people have busy lives that require flexibility, and these plans are inflexible. So, instead of a plan, we offer 5 guidelines for triathletes. If you follow these guidelines as closely as possible, you'll be amazed at how energetic, strong and focused you start to feel. And if you're carrying a few extra pounds, you might be startled to see them starting to melt away as well!

That said, sometimes special accommodations need to be made for allergies, digestive issues and other health problems. If you have special dietary needs, always consult with a health care professional before making major diet alterations.

Guideline 1: Breakfast is Your Friend

We've all heard it a thousand times: breakfast is the most important meal of the day. Well, do you know why you've heard it so often? Because it is true! If you're a breakfast skipper, stop now! Breakfast stokes your metabolic fire and gets you ready to face the day and to train effectively. Here are some options for a great breakfast:

- 2 eggs, turkey sausage and a piece of whole-grain toast
- Whole grain toast with natural peanut butter
- Oatmeal with fresh berries
- Small bowl of whole-grain cereal with ½ grapefruit
- Egg white omelet with asparagus, mushrooms and low-fat cheese
- Greek yogurt with fresh berries and a sprinkling of granola

Guideline 2: Cut Them OUT

Everyone has a cheat day from time to time. However if you get these things out of your house, you're far less likely to indulge in them regularly, and they instead become the occasional treat while out. Get these foods out of your house for the duration of your training program:

- Refined sugar
- Pop
- Candy
- Potato chips
- White bread, pasta, and other products made with refined flour

Guideline 3: Would Your Great Grandmother Recognize It?

This is a great piece of general diet advice. If your (or someone else's, we realize people have different cultural and dietary backgrounds) wouldn't recognize something as food, throw it out.

That means that things like meat, vegetables and fruits are good. Things that have been refined, processed, sealed in bags or frozen in tiny inedible individual portions, are bad.

Guideline 4: Shop the Outsides

If you go to your average grocery store, almost all of the good food is contained on the outer aisles. If you stay away from the middle, you can't go too far wrong. This means that when you shop you should look for:

- Fresh meat
- Fresh fruits and vegetables
- Whole grains
- Low-fat dairy

It's pretty simple, isn't it?

Guideline 5: Post Training Nutrition

After you're finished training on any given day, you should eat or drink something to help your body recover. Recovery is the most important part of the training process (more on that later) and by giving your body the right ingredients, it can rebuild itself stronger, faster and healthier after each session. Good recovery snacks and drinks include:

- Chocolate milk (my personal #1 pick)
- Greek yogurt
- Hummus on some pita bread
- Small protein shake
- Lean turkey on wholegrain bread

If you follow these nutritional guidelines, you can be sure that you're giving your body the energy it needs to get through the next four weeks. Remember, don't try to short yourself on calories when training. If you do that in some sort of misguided attempt to lose weight, you'll just end up feeling listless and non-energetic. Instead, focus on getting good calories from high-value food sources.

PRO TIP – Eat a healthy snack once or twice a day between meals to keep your metabolism running high. Yep, that's right, if you want to lose some weight, eat more, not less!

Chapter 4: Week 1: Am I Crazy?

The goal of this week is just to get your body used to alternating your training styles, and incorporating all three elements of the triathlon into your exercise program. In addition, we're going to incorporate strength training and flexibility elements into the program. This helps improve your performance and prevent injury, and will make you an overall fitter person.

A final word of caution: ALL exercise programs should be cleared with your doctor before you begin. Strenuous exercise is healthy for most people, but if you have preexisting health conditions such as asthma, diabetes or heart disease, you need to discuss training with your doctor before diving in.

That said, let's get started!

Day 1

- ½ hour run
- Resistance: Upper Body (light) workout

On this first ½ hour run, it's not about speed, it's not about the race and it's not about improving. Instead, think of it as a gauge of where you're at in your fitness level. If you find running for a ½ hour straight difficult, don't despair! Instead, alternate running and walking in any interval that you need to in order to get through the run. So if you find the run:

- Very Hard: Try walking 4 minutes running 2 (5 times)
- Hard: Try walking 3 minutes running 3 minutes (5 times)
- Difficult: Try walking 2 minutes running 4 minutes (5 times)
- Slightly Challenging: Run 5 minutes walk 1 (5 times)

For your resistance workout on this day and throughout the program, keep the weight light, and concentrate on good form over higher weight or more reps. You should be able to do 12 reps at a given weight on your first day. If you can't, move to a lighter weight.

The exact exercises you do when resistance training depend on your previous level of experience. By all means use other exercises if you're more confident with free weights or have good technique in a variety of exercises. But here is a sample program:

- Pushups (3 sets of 10)
- Bench Press (3 sets of 12 reps)
- Triceps Extension (3X12)
- Military Press (3X12)
- Hammer Curl (3X12)
- Bent Over Dumbbell Row (3X12)

Day 2

- Rest

Now, it is important to realize that rest means exactly that. You can do some light stretching or go for a walk by all means, but don't think that by sneaking in an extra workout that you're going to progress faster in your training program. Instead, you'll actually set yourself back.

Your rest days are the most important part of your program. This is because this is the day that your body heals and rebuilds itself stronger than it was before your last workout. Without proper rest, you just wear down your body and cause injuries. In fact, without rest, the untrained athlete stands a very good chance of never completing their first sprint triathlon. However, if you respect your rest days and follow the problem, we have every bit of confidence that you're going to cross that finish line.

Day 3

- Swim: 10 X 50 M lengths
- Resistance: Legs (light)

PRO TIP - If you're not an experienced swimmer, then you may find this the most difficult part of the training program. If you haven't swum in years, then you should get some swimming instruction at least once a week. Refresh your memory on the basic strokes and figure out which one works best for your current abilities.

The same rules here and throughout the program as with the first upper body workout. If you have exercises you prefer, or access to equipment that provides other leg workout options, feel free to try them. The goal here is just to get a good strength training session in on your lower body.

- Squats (3X12)
- Lunges (3X12)
- Split Squats (3X12)
- Calf Raises (3X12)
- Leg Press (3X12)
- Leg Curl (3X12)

Day 4

- Rest

Day 5

- Cycle: 30 Minutes
- Flexibility: Yoga

Yoga has been proven to deliver results to athletes of all stripes. Although a single class per week won't really boost your results through the roof, it is perfect for relaxing your body and helping you to stay supple, flexible and injury free. Even NFL players (and ex-players such as Michael Strahan) have come forward and talked about how much benefit they've seen from incorporating Yoga into their workout programs.

Day 6

- Rest

Day 7

- Run: 25 Minutes
- Bike: 20 Minutes

This is the day where we start to combine the different exercises that make up a triathlon. Again, if you're finding the run difficult, don't be afraid to run and walk. If the bike is hard, vary your pace, but push through it. On the other side of all this pain is your first completed triathlon! You can take a rest between these two workouts, but the closer together you can put them, the better!

Chapter 5: Week 2: Putting the Puzzle Together

In week 2, your goal is to focus on training sessions that up the ante and combine 2 of your training activities each workout day. We're also upping your workout days to 4. Maintain proper nutrition and, if the training sessions are getting tough or you're having a hard time staying focused, don't be afraid to jump to the next chapter and read about the mental challenges of triathlon training.

This week is pretty straightforward, in that you're just trying to get used to doing varied activities in a single day. If you can get your swim/bike, bike/run and run/swim combination scheduled as closely together as possible, that will pay dividends at the end of the program.

Day 1

- Run: 30 Minutes
- Bike: 30 Minutes
- Resistance: Upper Body
- Pushups (3X10)
- Triceps Extensions (3X12)
- Bench Press (3X12)
- Hammer Curl (3X12)

- Dumbbell Overhead Press (3X12)
- Upright Row (3X12)

Day 2

- Rest

PRO TIP - Flexibility isn't just for your stretching days. On every day before your workout you should take ten minutes to stretch your body out thoroughly. Work from head to toe and try to stretch out all of your major muscle groups. Doing so will really help you avoid injury later on.

Day 3

- Bike: 35 Minutes
- Swim: 10 X 50 M Lengths
- Flexibility or Yoga Session

Day 4

- Rest

Day 5

- Run: 30 Minutes
- Swim: 10 X 50 M
- Resistance: Lower Body
- Squats (3X12)
- Lunges (3X12)
- Goblet Squat (3X12)
- Leg Press (3X12)
- Calf Raise (3X12)
- Split Squats (3X12)

By the end of your second week, you want to have settled on which swimming stroke you're actually going to use in the race. For the last two weeks of training, you should focus on that stroke during your swim days. If you're a beginner and have been taking lessons, talk to your swim coach about which stroke is going to be best for you. If you're a more experienced swimmer and feel confident using any stroke, you probably want to use the front crawl. However, if you find completing the distance difficult, you can always roll over to backstroke for a short period of time, then switch back. Backstroke is a slower way to swim, but also takes less effort and can be a way to recover mid-race.

Day 6

- Rest

Day 7

- Run: 35 Minutes
- Bike: 35 Minutes

Chapter 6: Keeping Your Head on Straight: The Mental Side of Triathlons

Many people don't think about how hard this kind of challenge can be mentally. When you start putting your body through a new training program, there are several different ways that your mind might react. First, and most common, is that it might tell you to quit. This is a terrible thing to go through, but it happens to the best of us.

The truth is that it is hard to break habits. When the schedule says it's time to go for a run, there is always going to be some part of your brain suggesting that sitting on the couch and eating ice cream would be far preferable. This is because you've trained your brain through years and years of bad habits that these are the most pleasurable behaviors available to you, and the brain seeks and demands pleasure with an insistence that is sometimes hard to ignore!

However, exercise releases large amounts of endorphins into the body. These are chemicals in the body that control and influence our feelings of well being. If you can stick with your program through this month, you will find that you've actually retrained your brain to understand that exercise and training brings you pleasure! In addition, you'll find that the sense of accomplishment you get when you complete your sprint triathlon is a hundred times more satisfying than some rocky road and the latest season of Survivor.

PRO TIP - Get a buddy to train with! Despite the fact that it's basically common knowledge now that training with a buddy helps keep you on track and motivated, it is amazing how many people still don't do it! Training with a friend keeps you motivated, challenged and accountable to each other!

The Dark Side

There is a serious mental mistake that can be made on the other side of training. I think of this as the dark side, because no one wants to admit that they would do it, and yet so many people do. This is over-training, not resting properly or ignoring injuries.

The thing about increasing your fitness and your competitive ability as an athlete is that you want it to be a life-long pursuit. By not letting your body heal properly, you're putting all of that in serious jeopardy. You've heard about 'playing through the pain' and 'feeling the burn' but there is a very real danger of taking this mindset too far.

Training is hard; there is no doubt about it. You will feel uncomfortable, for sure. But there is a big difference between discomfort and pain. If you feel pain you need to stop. Pain is one of the most wonderful tools the body has. It is the body's check engine light. If it hurts, your body is saying that you need to park it and let it rest for a while; otherwise you could do serious damage.

If you experience an injury or any extreme discomfort, dizziness, shortness of breath or chest pains during your training, you need to stop. See a doctor. With the right medical help and advice, you can find ways to continue to train no matter what your health issues may be, but if you don't seek medical advice when you need to because you want to be 'tough' or a 'winner' you stand the risk of doing yourself serious damage.

Staying Focused

The final piece of mental advice applies to training sessions, but certainly also to the race itself. You're going to experience a lot of intense emotions during the race, ranging from excitement, to frustration, to exhaustion to, hopefully, elation. You're going to feel like quitting at times. But stay focused on the short term goals. Just concentrate on the next mile, the next step or the next stroke. Remember that you did the training and put in the work, and that you can do it.

When you cross the finish line, it will all be worth it.

Chapter 7: Week 3: Stepping, Pedaling and Stroking It Up a Notch

In week 3, it is time to start trying to improve your speed. We'll carry this training method through to week 4. You're going to accomplish this by alternating your intensity during each of your workouts. The reason for this is that if you simply finish the workouts and never push your speed, you'll have a difficult time improving beyond your ability to simply finish the race, although your strength training also helps with increasing speed.

This week also comes with only 2 rest days, but the variance of the exercise being done should still give your body the time it needs to recover.

Day 1

- Rest

Remember that we worked out in day 7 of week 2. Although it might feel strange to start a week on a rest day, this is necessary after what you've been through up until this point!

Day 2

- Run: 40 Minutes
- Swim: 12 X 50 M

Alternating intensity is the watchword this week. This means that you're going to switch up how much effort you're putting into your run and swim throughout the workout. This same principle will apply to your swimming and biking on day 4 and your bike and swim on day 5.

Here's a sample division of the run. Apply similar principles to the varying length workouts and to the bike-ride.

- 5 minutes – easy jog
- 5 minutes – moderate jog
- 5 minutes – run
- 2 minutes – sprint
- 5 minutes - moderate jog
- 2 minutes – sprint
- 6 minutes – moderate jog

When you push your body to the maximum speed it can achieve in a given exercise, you're helping to push it beyond your current level of fitness. This is where you can truly start to get faster at a given part of the race, rather than simply training for the endurance to complete it.

Day 3

- Resistance: Whole Body

Sample Workout:

- Pushups (3X12)
- Squats (3X12)
- Bench Press (3X12)
- Lunges (3X12)
- Crunches (3X12)
- Calf Raises (3X12)
- Military Press (3X12)
- Triceps Extensions (3X12)

Day 4

- Swim: 12 X 50 M
- Bike: 40 Minutes

Day 5

- Run: 50 Minutes
- Resistance: Whole Body

Sample Workout:

- Decline Pushups (3X12)
- Goblet Squats (3X12)
- Wide Grip Bench Press (3X12)
- Lunges (3X12)
- Crunches (3X12)
- Calf Raises (3X12)
- Military Press (3X12)
- Triceps Extensions (3X12)
- Split Squats (3X12)

Day 6

- Bike: 40 Minutes
- Swim: 12 X 50 M

Day 7

- Rest

Chapter 8: Week 4: The Final Stretch

Okay, this is it. If you've made it this far you've already accomplished a lot. All you have to do now is stick with the last few days of training and then reap the benefits by completing your very first sprint triathlon. The first day of this week is the most important. This is your first time trying all three of your activities together. If this is hard, confusing or exhausting, don't worry. It is supposed to be! But just remember that this is your own, private, first triathlon, and that it is an achievement all on its own.

Day 1

- Swim: 12 X 50 M
- Bike: 40 Minutes
- Run: 40 Minutes

Try to schedule these 3 activities as close to back to back as you can. You want to try and mimic the conditions of your triathlon as closely as you can. Get used to the idea that you're fit enough to do this! After three weeks of work, you are ready for the triathlon, it is just a matter of putting it all together.

Day 2

- Stretch

This is a great day for Yoga, tai chi or other gentle activities that stimulate increased flexibility and blood flow. It is good to realize the part these types of activities and gentle walking can play in recovery. They improve circulation and get the blood pumping to your body without putting extreme extra stress on it. This is helpful for recovery.

PRO TIP – When looking for a Yoga class or video to do on your off days, don't look for things like 'power' or 'hot' yoga. These workouts, especially for someone who is not experienced with yoga, can be just as taxing as your runs. Look for something a little gentler like a gentle hatha or restorative Yoga class instead.

Day 3

- Run: 45 Minutes
- Swim: 12 X 50 M

Day 4

- Resistance: Whole Body
- Biking: 50 Minutes

Sample Workout:

- Pushups (3X12)
- Squats (3X12)
- Bench Press (3X12)
- Lunges (3X12)
- Crunches (3X12)
- Calf Raises (3X12)
- Military Press (3X12)
- Triceps Extensions (3X12)

Day 5

- Run: 30 Minutes
- Bike: 30 Minutes
- Swim: 10 X 50 M

Day 6

- Rest

Day 7

- Race

This is it! The big day! You've made it. Of course, you still have to get through the race. Here are a couple of tips to help you make it.

- Get proper nutrition the night before, and on the morning of your race. Pasta the night before a race is a good standard, and oatmeal makes for a filling breakfast that will provide you with the energy you need to get through.

- Pay special attention to your hydration in the days leading up to the race. You want to be sure your fluids are up before the race, because they will certainly be depleted afterwards.

Congratulations! You made it, and we hope you enjoyed your training program, and the completion of your first race. However, the book's not over yet. We have a few more things for you to think about, including injury care, and what comes next!

Chapter 9: Injuries: The Broken, The Battered, and The Bruised

If you hurt yourself during your training, it is critical that you look after yourself properly. If you do this, it not only reduces the chance of further and more serious injury, it also increases the odds that you'll be able to get back to training and complete your race as scheduled!

Stress Injury

This is the most common type of injury for triathletes. It is the result of repetitive movement on joints that can't properly absorb the force being applied to them. For these types of injuries, you want to utilize the RICE method of care.

- R: Rest
- I: Ice
- C: Compression
- E: Elevate

This basic treatment strategy applied often and early will help you heal before small injuries can turn into big ones.

Sprains, Twists, and Pulls

These are also common issues for triathletes. RICE can be applied again, but if you notice ongoing pain, significant bruising, or swelling, then it is time to go see your doctor.

Dehydration

This is an insidious problem that many triathletes don't account for properly. There is something about spending time in a pool that tends to make people forget that dehydration is a real risk. Be sure to drink plenty of water, and if you have a particularly strenuous workout, some sports drink to replenish electrolytes is also a good idea.

Chapter 10: What's Next: Diving Back in Again!

Congratulations! If you've made it to this point then you've completed your very first sprint triathlon! Take a moment and enjoy your feeling of victory... but just a moment!

Now it is time to move onto the next challenge. Typically, there are two options from here:

- Try to reduce your sprint time

- Move up to the next category of triathlon

Either of these is a great option, but require slightly different approaches to training.

First of all, before beginning your next training program, be sure to give yourself some time off. You've just completed a very rigorous training program and you should give your body at least a week to recover. Feel free to go for an easy jog or do yoga during that week but, other than that, just relax, eat healthy and let your body heal.

Then it's time to get back in the saddle! If you want to lower your sprint time, you need to concentrate on sprinting more during your endurance workouts and increasing the amount of strength training you're doing. Many people underestimate the part that strength training plays in speed, but it is a critical training component, especially when trying to increase speed over relatively short distances.

If you're looking to move up to an Olympic length triathlon, then good on you! This next level of training is going to be harder and require more from you. Leave yourself a much longer training period, 12-16 weeks is a good idea, before your longer triathlon. Even if you started from scratch, the increase in fitness required between a sprint and an Olympic triathlon is greater than the change you've made since you opened this book to complete your first sprint.

However, the principles remain the same. Remember:

- Fuel your body

- Do the training

- Get your rest

Stick to those basic ideals, and you'll tackle your next

triathlon whether it is a sprint, Olympic, half-ironman or ironman with the recuperation you need!

Chapter 11: Other Recommended Resources

Here are some additional resources that I think you may find useful:

"WILLPOWER: How to Achieve Your Goals by Making a Plan and Sticking to It with Self-Control, Discipline, and Ease"

http://www.amazon.com/dp/B00LH9NJZG/

People often blame the lack of their own willpower as one of the key barriers to change, thus preventing them from achieving their own life goals. The inability to discipline and control one's self often results in faulty choices and poor decisions. Goal-setting may be a good starting point in working towards your goals, but if you can't stick to the plan with the right amount of discipline and willpower, then achieving those goals will be a difficult task. This book will explain what willpower is, how it works, and gives you specific advice on how to strengthen your willpower to achieve your life goals.

"Mental Toughness: The Ultimate Performance Guide for the Elite Athlete"

http://www.amazon.com/dp/B00LW1X7UG/

Any physical superiority an elite athlete may (or may not) be naturally gifted with MUST be accompanied with severe discipline and a mental toughness that cannot be fathomed by people who aren't trained the same way. Your physical capabilities, no matter how great, will not keep you at the top, rather it's your discipline and mental toughness that allows you to keep charging forth even when your own body appears to be working against you. How do you keep training when all your physical strength is drained? And how do you maintain strict workout routines even after you know you're without a doubt the very best at your field? That is what this book will reveal. It will teach you how to resist slacking off, and how to become the master of your own mind such that even your body will not rebel against what you have conceived in your mind. The essence of this book is to reveal how you can unravel your inner drive... the drive which makes champions even greater... the drive from which all elite athletes are made of.

"Breaking Bad Habits: How to Break a Bad Habit and Introduce Good New Habits for Health, Wealth, & Happiness"

http://www.amazon.com/dp/B00LU7K5NE/

Habits are very powerful factors in a person's life. Knowing how to invest in good habits can lead to your success, while failing to remove bad habits can lead to your own demise. This book will guide you from being able to control and eliminate your bad habits to establishing new productive habits using simple steps and techniques including the 'bait and switch' method, the 'habit stacking' method, and many more!

Made in the USA
San Bernardino,
CA

58512121R00038